THE JPS B'NAI MITZVAH TORAH COMMENTARY

Lekh Lekha (Genesis 12:1–17:27)
Haftarah (Isaiah 40:27–41:16)

Rabbi Jeffrey K. Salkin

The Jewish Publication Society · Philadelphia
University of Nebraska Press · Lincoln

INTRODUCTION

News flash: the most important thing about becoming bar or bat mitzvah isn't the party. Nor is it the presents. Nor even being able to celebrate with your family and friends—as wonderful as those things are. Nor is it even standing before the congregation and reading the prayers of the liturgy—as important as that is.

No, the most important thing about becoming bar or bat mitzvah is sharing Torah with the congregation. And why is that? Because of all Jewish skills, that is the most important one.

Here is what is true about rites of passage: you can tell what a culture values by the tasks it asks its young people to perform on their way to maturity. In American culture, you become responsible for driving, responsible for voting, and yes, responsible for drinking responsibly.

In some cultures, the rite of passage toward maturity includes some kind of trial, or a test of strength. Sometimes, it is a kind of "outward bound" camping adventure. Among the Maasai tribe in Africa, it is traditional for a young person to hunt and kill a lion. In some Hispanic cultures, fifteen year-old girls celebrate the *quinceañera*, which marks their entrance into maturity.

What is Judaism's way of marking maturity? It combines both of these rites of passage: *responsibility* and *test*. You show that you are on your way to becoming a *responsible* Jewish adult through a public *test* of strength and knowledge—reading or chanting Torah, and then teaching it to the congregation.

This is the most important Jewish ritual mitzvah (commandment), and that is how you demonstrate that you are, truly, bar or bat mitzvah—old enough to be responsible for the mitzvot.

What Is Torah?

So, what exactly is the Torah? You probably know this already, but let's review.

The Torah (teaching) consists of "the five books of Moses," sometimes also called the *chumash* (from the Hebrew word *chameish,* which means "five"), or, sometimes, the Greek word Pentateuch (which means "the five teachings").

Here are the five books of the Torah, with their common names and their Hebrew names.

> **Genesis (The beginning), which in Hebrew is Bere'shit (from the first words—"When God began to create").** Bere'shit spans the years from Creation to Joseph's death in Egypt. Many of the Bible's best stories are in Genesis: the creation story itself; Adam and Eve in the Garden of Eden; Cain and Abel; Noah and the Flood; and the tales of the Patriarchs and Matriarchs, Abraham, Isaac, Jacob, Sarah, Rebekah, Rachel, and Leah. It also includes one of the greatest pieces of world literature, the story of Joseph, which is actually the oldest complete novel in history, comprising more than one-quarter of all Genesis.

> **Exodus (Getting out), which in Hebrew is Shemot (These are the names).** Exodus begins with the story of the Israelite slavery in Egypt. It then moves to the rise of Moses as a leader, and the Israelites' liberation from slavery. After the Israelites leave Egypt, they experience the miracle of the parting of the Sea of Reeds (or "Red Sea"); the giving of the Ten Commandments at Mount Sinai; the idolatry of the Golden Calf; and the design and construction of the Tabernacle and of the ark for the original tablets of the law, which our ancestors carried with them in the desert. Exodus also includes various ethical and civil laws, such as "You shall not wrong a stranger or oppress him, for you were strangers in the land of Egypt" (22:20).

> **Leviticus (about the Levites), or, in Hebrew, Va-yikra' (And God called).** It goes into great detail about the kinds of sacrifices that the ancient Israelites brought as offerings; the laws of ritual purity; the animals that were permitted and forbidden for eating (the beginnings of the tradition of kashrut, the Jewish dietary laws); the diagnosis of various skin diseases; the ethical laws of holiness; the ritual calendar of the Jewish year; and various agricultural laws concerning the treatment of the Land of Israel. Leviticus is basically the manual of ancient Judaism.

> Numbers (because the book begins with the census of the Isra-
elites), or, in Hebrew, Be-midbar (In the wilderness). The book
describes the forty years of wandering in the wilderness and the
various rebellions against Moses. The constant theme: "Egypt
wasn't so bad. Maybe we should go back." The greatest rebellion
against Moses was the negative reports of the spies about the
Land of Israel, which discouraged the Israelites from wanting to
move forward into the land. For that reason, the "wilderness generation" must die off before a new generation can come into maturity and finish the journey.

> Deuteronomy (The repetition of the laws of the Torah), or, in
Hebrew, Devarim (The words). The final book of the Torah is,
essentially, Moses's farewell address to the Israelites as they pre-
pare to enter the Land of Israel. Here we find various laws that
had been previously taught, though sometimes with different
wording. Much of Deuteronomy contains laws that will be important to the Israelites as they enter the Land of Israel—laws
concerning the establishment of a monarchy and the ethics of
warfare. Perhaps the most famous passage from Deuteronomy
contains the *Shema*, the declaration of God's unity and unique-
ness, and the *Ve-ahavta*, which follows it. Deuteronomy ends with
the death of Moses on Mount Nebo as he looks across the Jordan
Valley into the land that he will not enter.

Jews read the Torah in sequence—starting with Bere'shit right after Simchat Torah in the autumn, and then finishing Devarim on the
following Simchat Torah. Each Torah portion is called a parashah (di-
vision; sometimes called a *sidrah*, a place in the order of the Torah
reading). The stories go around in a full circle, reminding us that we
can always gain more insights and more wisdom from the Torah. This
means that if you don't "get" the meaning this year, don't worry—it
will come around again.

And What Else? The Haftarah

We read or chant the Torah from the Torah scroll—the most sacred
thing that a Jewish community has in its possession. The Torah is

written without vowels, and the ability to read it and chant it is part of the challenge and the test.

But there is more to the synagogue reading. Every Torah reading has an accompanying haftarah reading. Haftarah means "conclusion," because there was once a time when the service actually ended with that reading. Some scholars believe that the reading of the haftarah originated at a time when non-Jewish authorities outlawed the reading of the Torah, and the Jews read the haftarah sections instead. In fact, in some synagogues, young people who become bar or bat mitzvah read very little Torah and instead read the entire haftarah portion.

The haftarah portion comes from the Nevi'im, the prophetic books, which are the second part of the Jewish Bible. It is either read or chanted from a Hebrew Bible, or maybe from a booklet or a photocopy.

The ancient sages chose the haftarah passages because their themes reminded them of the words or stories in the Torah text. Sometimes, they chose *haftarah* with special themes in honor of a festival or an upcoming festival.

Not all books in the prophetic section of the Hebrew Bible consist of prophecy. Several are historical. For example:

The book of Joshua tells the story of the conquest and settlement of Israel.

The book of Judges speaks of the period of early tribal rulers who would rise to power, usually for the purpose of uniting the tribes in war against their enemies. Some of these leaders are famous: Deborah, the great prophetess and military leader, and Samson, the biblical strong man.

The books of Samuel start with Samuel, the last judge, and then move to the creation of the Israelite monarchy under Saul and David (approximately 1000 BCE).

The books of Kings tell of the death of King David, the rise of King Solomon, and how the Israelite kingdom split into the Northern Kingdom of Israel and the Southern Kingdom of Judah (approximately 900 BCE).

And then there are the books of the prophets, those spokesmen for God whose words fired the Jewish conscience. Their names are immortal: Isaiah, Jeremiah, Ezekiel, Amos, Hosea, among others.

Someone once said: "There is no evidence of a biblical prophet ever being invited back a second time for dinner." Why? Because the prophets were tough. They had no patience for injustice, apathy, or hypocrisy. No one escaped their criticisms. Here's what they taught:

› God commands the Jews to behave decently toward one another. In fact, God cares more about basic ethics and decency than about ritual behavior.
› God chose the Jews *not* for special privileges, but for special duties to humanity.
› As bad as the Jews sometimes were, there was always the possibility that they would improve their behavior.
› As bad as things might be now, it will not always be that way. Someday, there will be universal justice and peace. Human history is moving forward toward an ultimate conclusion that some call the Messianic Age: a time of universal peace and prosperity for the Jewish people and for all the people of the world.

Your Mission—To Teach Torah to the Congregation

On the day when you become bar or bat mitzvah, you will be reading, or chanting, Torah—in Hebrew. You will be reading, or chanting, the haftarah—in Hebrew. That is the major skill that publicly marks the becoming of bar or bat mitzvah. But, perhaps even more important than that, you need to be able to teach something about the Torah portion, and perhaps the haftarah as well.

And that is where this book comes in. It will be a very valuable resource for you, and your family, in the b'nai mitzvah process.

Here is what you will find in it:

› A brief **summary** of every Torah portion. This is a basic overview of the portion; and, while it might not refer to everything in the Torah portion, it will explain its most important aspects.
› A list of the **major ideas** in the Torah portion. The purpose: to make the Torah portion real, in ways that we can relate to. Every Torah portion contains unique ideas, and when you put all

of those ideas together, you actually come up with a list of Judaism's most important ideas.

> Two ***divrei Torah*** ("words of Torah," or "sermonettes") for each portion. These *divrei Torah* explain significant aspects of the Torah portion in accessible, reader-friendly language. Each *devar Torah* contains references to **traditional** Jewish sources (those that were written before the modern era), as well as **modern** sources and quotes. We have searched, far and wide, to find sources that are unusual, interesting, and not just the "same old stuff" that many people already know about the Torah portion. Why did we include these minisermons in the volume? Not because we want you to simply copy those sermons and pass them off as your own (that would be cheating), though you are free to quote from them. We included them so that you can see what is possible— how you can try to make meaning for yourself out of the words of Torah.

> **Connections:** This is perhaps the most valuable part. It's a list of questions that you can ask yourself, or that others might help you think about—any of which can lead to the creation of your *devar Torah.*

Note: you don't have to like everything that's in a particular Torah portion. Some aren't that loveable. Some are hard to understand; some are about religious practices that people today might find confusing, and even offensive; some contain ideas that we might find totally outmoded.

But this doesn't have to get in the way. After all, most kids spend a lot of time thinking about stories that contain ideas that modern people would find totally bizarre. Any good medieval fantasy story falls into that category.

And we also believe that, if you spend just a little bit of time with those texts, you can begin to understand what the author was trying to say.

This volume goes one step further. Sometimes, the haftarah comes off as a second thought, and no one really thinks about it. We have tried to solve that problem by including a **summary** of each haftarah, and then a mini-sermon on the haftarah. This will help you learn how these sacred words are relevant to today's world, and even to your own life.

All Bible quotations come from the NJPS translation, which is found in the many different editions of the JPS TANAKH; in the Conservative movement's *Etz Hayim: Torah and Commentary;* in the Reform movement's *Torah: A Modern Commentary;* and in other Bible commentaries and study guides.

How Do I Write a *Devar Torah?*

It really is easier than it looks.

There are many ways of thinking about the *devar Torah.* It is, of course, a short sermon on the meaning of the Torah (and, perhaps, the haftarah) portion. It might even be helpful to think of the *devar Torah* as a "book report" on the portion itself.

The most important thing you can know about this sacred task is: *Learn* the words. *Love* the words. Teach people what it could mean to *live* the words.

Here's a basic outline for a *devar Torah:*

"My Torah portion is (name of portion)_____,
   from the book of _____, chapter
   _____.

"In my Torah portion, we learn that_____
   (Summary of portion)

"For me, the most important lesson of this Torah portion is (what is the best thing in the portion? Take the portion as a whole; your *devar Torah* does not have to be only, or specifically, on the verses that you are reading).

"As I learned my Torah portion, I found myself wondering:

› *Raise a question that the Torah portion itself raises.*
› *"Pick a fight"* with the portion. Argue with it.
› *Answer a question* that is listed in the "Connections" section of each Torah portion.
› *Suggest a question to your rabbi* that you would want the rabbi to answer in his or her own *devar Torah* or sermon.

"I have lived the values of the Torah by _____
(here, you can talk about how the Torah portion relates to your
own life. If you have done a mitzvah project, you can talk about
that here).

How To Keep It from Being Boring
(and You from Being Bored)

Some people just don't like giving traditional speeches. From our perspective, that's really okay. Perhaps you can teach Torah in a different way—one that makes sense to you.

> ⟩ Write an "open letter" to one of the characters in your Torah portion. "Dear Abraham: I hope that your trip to Canaan was not too hard . . ." "Dear Moses: Were you afraid when you got the Ten Commandments on Mount Sinai? I sure would have been . . ."
> ⟩ Write a news story about what happens. Imagine yourself to be a television or news reporter. "Residents of neighboring cities were horrified yesterday as the wicked cities of Sodom and Gomorrah were burned to the ground. Some say that God was responsible . . ."
> ⟩ Write an imaginary interview with a character in your Torah portion.
> ⟩ Tell the story from the point of view of another character, or a minor character, in the story. For instance, tell the story of the Garden of Eden from the point of view of the serpent. Or the story of the Binding of Isaac from the point of view of the ram, which was substituted for Isaac as a sacrifice. Or perhaps the story of the sale of Joseph from the point of view of his coat, which was stripped off him and dipped in a goat's blood.
> ⟩ Write a poem about your Torah portion.
> ⟩ Write a song about your Torah portion.
> ⟩ Write a play about your Torah portion, and have some friends act it out with you.
> ⟩ Create a piece of artwork about your Torah portion.

The bottom line is: Make this a joyful experience. Yes—it could even be fun.

The Very Last Thing You Need to Know at This Point

The Torah scroll is written without vowels. Why? Don't *sofrim* (Torah scribes) know the vowels?

Of course they do.

So, why do they leave the vowels out?

One reason is that the Torah came into existence at a time when sages were still arguing about the proper vowels, and the proper pronunciation.

But here is another reason: The Torah text, as we have it today, and as it sits in the scroll, is actually *an unfinished work*. Think of it: the words are just sitting there. Because they have no vowels, it is as if they have no voice.

When we read the Torah publicly, we give voice to the ancient words. And when we find meaning in those ancient words, and we talk about those meanings, those words jump to life. They enter our lives. They make our world deeper and better.

Mazal tov to you, and your family. This is your journey toward Jewish maturity. Love it.

THE TORAH

❖ Lekh Lekha: Genesis 12:1–17:27

Things are not working out the way God wanted. Adam and Eve dis-
obeyed the divine order not to eat of the Tree of Knowledge of Good
and Evil. Cain killed Abel. People were so bad that God had to bring
a flood to the earth. Then, people got arrogant and built a tower in an
attempt to reach the heavens. Enough!

God decides to choose one man to become a holy person and be a
role model for how humans should really be.

This is how Jewish history begins: God tells Abram (Abraham) to say
goodbye to the place where he is living, Haran; to his father; and to everything he knows. Abram and his wife, Sarai (Sarah), wind up in the land of
Canaan (Israel)—but as soon as they get there, they go to Egypt to escape
famine. Sarai cannot have children, which poses challenges to Judaism's
"first family." She comes up with an interesting idea: Abraham should take
her slave, Hagar, and have children with her. Hagar gives birth to Ishmael.

Summary

› God commands Abram (Abraham) to leave his land and to go to the land that God would show him—the land of Canaan (Israel). (12:1–3)

› God tells Abraham that he, and the Jewish people, will be a blessing to the world, and that those who bless the Jewish people will be blessed, and that those who curse the Jewish people will be cursed. (12:1–9)

› In Egypt, Abram tries to pass Sarai off as his sister—with dangerous results. (12:10–20)

› Abram and his nephew, Lot, cannot get along, and so they divide the land of Canaan between them. (13:1–18)

› The Middle East has its first war, and Lot is taken hostage. Even though Abram has big problems with Lot, he goes out of his way to rescue him. (14:1–24)

› Abram has a bizarre dream in which God tells him that his people will be "strangers in a strange land"—not only in Egypt, but in many other places as well. (15:1–18)

The Big Ideas

> **Adventure is an essential part of life.** Jewish history starts with an adventure: Abram must leave everything that he knows, and go out into the great unknown. That means not only leaving a place; it means leaving old ideas behind, as well.

> **The mission of the Jewish people is to be a blessing to the world.** While Judaism is the religion of the Jewish people, the Jewish way of life has larger lessons that everyone can learn. This means, among many other things, modeling ethical behavior.

> **Lying is wrong—at least, most of the time.** Abram and Sarai are trapped in a ticklish situation in Egypt, and Abram feels he has to lie about Sarai and say that she is his sister. He is afraid that the Egyptians would kill him in order to take his wife from him. Sometimes, truth is not the largest value—saving life is.

> **All Jews are responsible for one another.** Abram has no warm and fuzzy feelings for his nephew, Lot. Still, when Lot is taken hostage, Abram has no choice but to act on his behalf and rescue him—traveling the length of the entire Land of Israel to do so. From this gesture we learn that even though the Jews are a small people, they are a very large family—and family feelings will always prevail. Jews have done this over and over again through the centuries, for example, saving fellow Jews during the Holocaust, Soviet Jews from Russia, and Ethiopian Jews from Ethiopia.

> **To be Jewish is to know what it means to be a stranger.** That was the essential message of the vision that Abram had—the "coming attractions" of his descendants becoming slaves in Egypt. The experience in Egypt taught the Jews the meaning of what it's like to be a stranger, and from this they learned to treat strangers with dignity.

Divrei Torah

WITHOUT A REBELLIOUS TEENAGER
THERE WOULD BE NO JEWS

If you were going to start a new religion, this might be what you would do: sit around thinking of great ideas and how to get others to believe in those ideas.

But that's not how the Jewish people began. Terah, the father of Abram (Abraham's original name) decided to move his family out of the city of Ur. Ur was the most sophisticated city of its time. It had great architecture, sculpture, and literature. It was the New York and Paris of 1800 BCE.

The family got as far as Haran, in what is today southern Turkey, and they decided to stay there. Then, suddenly, God told Abram that he had to get on the move again. He had to leave his land, and he had to leave his father, and that meant that he had to abandon his father's ways of looking at the world.

Who was Terah? What was he like? A famous legend teaches that Terah was in the idol business. It says that when Abram was thirteen years old he figured out that worshiping idols was wrong. He came up with an amazing realization: you can't make a god, because then you have power over the god that you have created—and then it can't be a god!

What did Abram do? According to a midrash, "Abram seized a stick, smashed all the images, and placed the stick in the hand of the biggest of them. When his father came, he asked: 'Who did this to the gods?' Abram answered: 'A woman came with a bowl of fine flour and said: "Here, offer it up to them." When I offered it, one god said, "I will eat first," and another said, "No, I will eat first." Then the biggest of them rose up and smashed all the others.' His father replied: 'Are you messing around with me? They cannot do anything!' Abram answered: 'You say they cannot. Let your ears hear what your mouth is saying!'"

As Jonathan Sacks, the former chief rabbi of Great Britain, writes: "There are times, especially in adolescence, when we tell ourselves that we are breaking with our parents, charting a path that is completely new."

And so, according to legend, Judaism began with a thirteen-year-old kid challenging the old ways of thinking. Jews challenge old ideas and create new ones. That has been one reason why so many great scientists, writers, and thinkers have been Jews. It has been the key to Jewish survival and creativity over the centuries.

THE JEWISH PEOPLE: WE ARE ALL IN IT TOGETHER

Let's face it—sometimes there are strange relationships in families.

Consider Abram and Lot. Lot was Abram's nephew, the son of Abram's brother, Haran (not to be confused with the city of Haran), who had died years before. After Haran died, Abram and Sarai were his only real family. And so, Abram took Lot with him when they began their journey to the land of Canaan (Israel). Abram always felt somewhat responsible for his nephew. He referred to Lot as his "brother," which in biblical times simply meant a close relative (13:8).

But, actually, Abram and Lot didn't get along. They were constantly arguing about who would own the land, and finally they decided to divide the land between them. Abram let Lot choose which land he wanted, and Lot chose the plush, fertile land in the Jordan Valley, near the wicked cities of Sodom and Gomorrah. Being near these places didn't bother Lot that much. His basic attitude toward life seemed to be "Whatever!" Lot and Abram were very different people, and when they physically separated from each other they became emotionally separated as well.

But then, in chapter 14. we find the first recorded war in the Torah. A coalition of four kings stage a rebellion against a coalition of five kings. In the midst of the war, one group of kings invades Sodom and Gomorrah, stealing all their food and taking Lot hostage. Abram gets an army together and pursues the enemy as far away as Damascus, which is very far away from where they were all living at the time. He rescues Lot and brings him back home. Abram already knew what the early sages would say, centuries later: "All Israel is responsible for one another."

Back in the beginning of Genesis, Cain had asked God: "Am I my brother's keeper?" (4:9). Abram knew the answer to that question. It is "yes." Jews don't have to like each other; they just have to care about each other. Abram knew that his responsibility for Lot was more important than his personal feelings for his nephew. According to Rabbi Joseph B. Soloveitchik: "A Jew must feel a duty to save his brother, even if his brother has departed from the righteous path. Loyalty is the first mark of Abraham."

Connections

> The forming of the Jewish people began with the act of going out into the unknown. Have you ever had that kind of experience: moving to a new house or community; going to a new camp, or a new school? What was it like? How do you think Abram must have felt?

> The Torah portion says that those nations that curse the Jewish people will themselves be cursed. In other words, countries that are good to the Jews will do well; if they don't, they will do badly. Is this true? Think of such examples as the Spanish Inquisition, the Russian pogroms, Nazi Germany, Arab countries' antisemitism. How has this pattern played out in history?

> Midrash says that Abram broke his father's idols. This means that Abram had the courage to break with what previous generations thought. How did people like Christopher Columbus, Charles Darwin, and Rosa Parks demonstrate that kind of courage? How have great Jewish women and men, like Albert Einstein, Hank Greenberg, Gloria Steinem, and Golda Meir, been courageous? What other names would you add to that list?

> According to tradition, Abram broke his father's idols at the age of thirteen, and that was one of the origins of bar mitzvah. This suggests that thirteen-year-olds are ready to think independently from their parents. In what ways do you disagree with your parents? How do you demonstrate that? When is it good for children to rebel against their parents? When is it not so good?

> Under what circumstances might it be permissible, and even necessary, to lie? Are "white lies" acceptable? For instances, is it okay to tell someone that you like his or her new shirt (or haircut, or whatever) when, in fact, you don't?

> How have Jews demonstrated their solidarity by helping other Jews? Think about such historical moments as the Holocaust and the rescuing of Jews from Russia and Ethiopia.

THE HAFTARAH

❖ Lekh Lekha: Isaiah 40:27–41:16

For someone who was anonymous, the prophet known as Second Isaiah certainly gets a lot of ink in the *haftarah*. Here he is again, speaking to the Judeans. His message is clear: despite the fact that they are in exile in Babylonia, they will soon be able to return to the Land of Israel—a move from despair to triumph. This will demonstrate God's power over history and over all the nations. God is the creator, the great victor, and the redeemer of Israel. God's power is revealed everywhere: in nature, in international affairs, and in the life of the Jewish people

Second Isaiah reminds Israel that they are the "seed of Abraham" (41:8), which forms the connection to the Torah portion. The Jews who were listening to Isaiah knew that God had made a great promise to Abraham. Believing that God would keep that promise and return them to the land of their ancestors gave the people hope in their time of exile.

Coming Home Again (or Why Jews Love Baseball)

How is the Bible like baseball? (Please don't say that they both start in the "big-inning"!) The purpose of baseball is that you start at home, and come home again.

And that is the message of Isaiah and a big lesson of the entire Hebrew Bible as well.

Let's review our history. In the year 586 BCE, Babylonian armies destroyed Jerusalem, burned the Temple, and deported the Judeans to Babylonia, thus beginning that period known as the Babylonian exile. Some years afterward, the Persian King Cyrus conquered Babylonia, and he let a group of Judeans return to the Land of Israel and rebuild the Temple. So, if you were wondering about the identity of the mysterious "victor from the East" in Isa. 41:2, it would be Cyrus, king of Persia, who was about to conquer Babylonia. That's the way it was in the ancient Middle East: every few hundred years the borders changed and you wound up living in a different empire.

According to the Bible: "The Lord roused the spirit of King Cyrus of Persia to issue a proclamation throughout his realm. . . . "The Lord God of Heaven has given me all the kingdoms of the earth and has charged me with building Him a house in Jerusalem, which is in Judah. Anyone of you of all His people—may his God be with him, and let him go up to Jerusalem that is in Judah . . . ; and all who stay behind, wherever he may be living, let the people of his place assist him with silver, gold, goods" (Ezra 1:1–4).

Cyrus asks everyone to help the Jews return to their land—with silver, gold, and goods. Where have we read that before? It is an echo of the Exodus from Egypt, when the Israelites asked their former Egyptian neighbors for silver and gold to take with them on their journey. The return to the Land of Israel is like an exodus from "another" Egypt—this time, from the Babylonian exile.

For Jews, Cyrus wins the award for Best Loved Foreign Ruler in the Ancient Middle East (though there wasn't that much competition). The Talmud notes that in Hebrew, Cyrus's name is Koresh (*kaph resh shin*), which contains the same letters as the word *kasher* (*kaph shin resh*), meaning "ritually fit and proper." Cyrus was kosher! Second Isaiah predicted that a Cyrus-like figure would help the Jews come home, although he probably did not live long enough to greet Cyrus as a hero. In our day, another hero helped the Jews return home. President Harry S. Truman gave crucial support to the Zionist cause and directed the United States to recognize the new Jewish state when the United Nations set it to a vote. Truman certainly helped create the State of Israel, but he thought that his role was even bigger than that. "What do you mean, 'helped create'? I am Cyrus, I am Cyrus!"

With those stirring words, Truman demonstrated that he was not only in favor of the creation of a Jewish state, but that he grounded that support in his belief in the ultimate truth of the ancient narrative. Truman read the Bible! He saw himself as the modern-day reincarnation of King Cyrus of Persia. And that was good news for the Jews who wanted to come home.

❖ Notes

❖ Notes